sky
bright
psalms

sky bright psalms
© Temple Cone and Cathexis Northwest Press

No part of this book may be reproduced without written permission of the publisher or author, except in reviews and articles.

First Printing: 2021

Paperback ISBN: 978-1-952869-26-6
Cover photo by Bryan Tollefson
Designed and edited by C. M. Tollefson

Cathexis Northwest Press

cathexisnorthwestpress.com

sky
bright
psalms

Poems by Temple Cone

Cathexis Northwest Press

Contents:

Burning Sappho	13

I.

Émigré	16
Paradiso	17
Death's Sparrow	19
Shake It Off, Just Shake It Off	21
Antipastoral	22
Southrenody	23
The Hawk You See May Be Your Own	24
Eclogue of the Wonder at the Resurrection of the Wheat	25
Polonaise	27

II.

What the Cave Painters Saw	30
What the Classics Teach	31
Some Folks Still Live by Myth	32
The Honey	33
Pomegranate	34
The Lyre	35
Sloth	36
Mister Wind	37
The Soldiers	38
The Day Would Be Remembered	39
Matchwood	40
We Have Invented Nothing	41
Quantum Novena	42
Salve	43
Falconry	44
De Caelis	45
A Conjecture Leading to a Psalm	46
Sortes Alabamae	47
Bending the Bow	48
Impressions	49
The Book of Clouds	51
A Closer Absence	52

III.

Gab and Briar	54
Lentecost	55

Oneliness	56
Parable, with Crawfish	57
Prophecy	58
Metonymic River	59
Axiom of Saturday Nights	60
Orchard	61
Covenant	62

For Angelyn Givens

Archer, arrow, bow, & mark

The clear sky has leaned against the wall.
It's like a prayer to the emptiness.
And the emptiness turns its face to us
and whispers,
I am not empty, I am open.

–Tomas Tranströmer

Burning Sappho

you burn me
— Sappho, fragment 38

First, understand
no one felt regret.
This tenth Muse,
whose limbs loosened
at a touch, melting
swift as tallow
into tears, sang
of slatterns and sluts,
made love a city pimp,
tricked out Psyche
in cheapest rouge.
She plucked hearts
easily as lyre strings,
mimicked, mocked
our secret hungers,
baring them to the light.
Even her papyri,
inked with characters
whose couplings
made the world
words, were flimsy
and tempting
as a woman's lace,
her scent everywhere,
her lovers, rejected
or forgotten,

clutching still at this prize
raiment and the body
echoing within.
It took days to gather
all her works.
Outside the library,
a harbor breeze
stirred the hems of robes,
breathed dust underfoot.
The bundles caught fast,
collapsed in sighs
of feathery smoke
with a singeing flash
whose memory lasts
longer than its burning.

I.

Émigré

Though no one is born in that city,

everyone who arrives there

by jet, steamer, highway, or train

hopes to be born. The names

of streets blossom on lips

like the tallies of saints.

There, one could join a game

of craps in a blind alley,

buy a roll of warm bread,

take a bit part in a new play,

eavesdrop on a broker

waiting for a taxi and learn

enough to take his job one day.

Yet a silence prevails amidst the fury

of cell phones and cargo trucks,

as if, as Rilke understood,

the whole world spoke from within

the sphere of its own solitude.

Trees of heaven sprout near steam vents.

A woman walks out of a shop

so gracefully one begins looking

for wings. And as afternoon sharpens

its guillotine light, a flourish

of piano notes tumbles

from a row house window

like the patter of raindrops

heard by a man too ill to leave

the brown confines of his room.

Paradiso

No blue grocery bags rustle
from the lindens
lining the freshly paved avenues.
No women stop before windows
to stare at mannequins
blank as angels.
A dog barks from a rose garden.
Motor scooters hurry, hummingbird-mad,
whenever the bright blossoms
of traffic lights turn green,
and the tanks everyone feared
would rumble in and shatter
grave- and cobblestones alike
languish in empty lots outside town,
peace having swept over them
in a storm of rust.
In the beginning, the minor chords
of waiters smoking outside
on red vinyl stools
or of alleyways shimmering
with a perpetual snowfall of pigeons
arranged moments one could live by.
But now, look how the butcher weeps
after calling the lamb to him,
after slitting its throat.
Look how the window-washers razor
white soap from the glass,
revealing a transparency so pure

they cannot peer inside.

And at the crossing

before the central bridge,

there's a red-tunicked officer,

his face chapped hard

as a falcon's from glaring into the wind,

who sends some across

and delays the rest

with the mere flick of his hand.

Death's Sparrow

In his twentieth-story apartment
Death keeps a fox sparrow he found
on the street corner one morning
during his rounds (lawyer, treadmill, coronary).
Sometime in the night, a hard wind
must have blown it from the nest
above the bank entrance.
There was a frieze,
something about workers, a shining leader
(president, oak desk, aneurism),
and when Death looked down,
he saw a furious, chattering ball
brown as gutter water,
murmured, *Now what's the fuss?*
and lifted the sparrow in his long hand.
At home, it hops around the kitchen,
talons clicking on linoleum,
eats seed from a bowl, but never truly flies,
not after chasing a sunset once
into the window overlooking the river.
He lets it perch on his thumb,
offers a cricket found in the hall.
He knows he ought to set it free
(park fountain, peregrine),
but his work's picking up this week
(a far island, earthquake),
the gray silence of the apartment
is terrifying sometimes,

and the sparrow's thin tail
taps his wrist as gently
as the ivory fan of a viscountess
(sleigh, wolves)
he knew many years ago.

Shake It Off, Just Shake It Off

Winter clouds line up
                like rosary beads—
clack, clack—against a Della Robbia-blue sky.
Mid-January's montage of tattered Christmania:
dry pines on street curbs,
                a wind-torn garland,
electric candles flickering at windows.

No one expects time to stay on her knees,
not the whitetails bounding uphill
or house wrens at the doorstep,
not the blown tamaracks, their seed cones
spilling over, and open.

The days, poor days: always with us,
till we notice dead bamboo more than green shoots,
till we accept the sum of our regrets
and wager we could spare
                a little ointment
from the sun's alabaster box.

I'd ante up,
        plunk down my one life
on the worn felt of this field,
more craps table
              than offertory plate, anyway,
for one roll of them bones, dotted with shadow,
while the clouds go looking on.

Antipastoral

Sure as bruises sweeten a pear,
the mountains' ozone haze ripens the day.

There's no pastoral here, just pesticide
drifting down in flurries upon sumac.

Surveyors prove the only visionaries:
over the baked blood of roadkill, they line

horizons with transit spirit levels.
Those who follow shall harrow the ground.

Southrenody

                    the ugliness

to crawl inside   to enmud
pay the vigorish   sapping sun

                    of the daily
                    of parched corn

amid the haze   make hay
the body's swerve   this landscape

                    Lucretian
                    a lapsed culture

a cissure   a caesura
with a mind   as clearcut

                    made wide
                    on a hill

not a jar   but beer cans
will engulf   big mouth big pour

                    the wilderness
                    so different

old town ladies   from the old men
maidens in halters   sullen

                    all the boys
                    come here

they say a man   wanting to letter us
to impaginate   each blue line

                    the whiteness
                    a vein at the wrist

a river   a cut in the land
what we show   to no one

                    we don't show

The Hawk You See May Be Your Own

A careful hawk's as good as a dead one.
Only when stooping from scrub pines,

pitched by hunger at shadows in the grass,
knows it its name, and nothing lonelier.

Same principle applies in calligraphy
and sighting a .308. Spit in your hand,

you can lift a burning branch from the fire
before you think about it, if you think about it.

Remember, and you'll know why a landscape
be it painted, parched, or snow-peaked,

so perfectly fits the wound in your heart.
Timberlines press their evergreens far north

into the everdark, amid the everwind,
because they've learned how to drink starlight.

It may take a hundred years or just a second
to see the hawk you see may be your own.

Eclogue of the Wonder at the Resurrection of the Wheat

Gonna make them wheatfields shine,
                               coos the sulky spring breeze
to her big sugar daddy, Sun,
                     him of the cottonmouth-thick wrists
and blue teardrop tats
                 back of each coal-webbed hand.
They lean against the Dodge,
                   side mirror like a pony's head
nuzzling both for sugar,
                   she all of sixteen, he of
you-know-better-than-to-ask.
                   If this be the resurrection
of forsythia-light after winter,
                   it'll take her juicy
kisses sluicing the cave
                   of his triple-earringed ear
to get things a-going,
                   for he's a brushfire not worth
walking ten feet to piss out,
                   beer belly like a brood sow's,
peachfuzz on his upper lip
                   like he don't know to wipe
his lips after peaches.
                   Still, this whole shebang's his gig.
She wants lightning, wants love,
                   and he's got ten gallons
of kerosene in the truck bed
                   with a sacred hunger to scorch

acres of gold into brass burn

                                  just for the savage wonder of it.

Polonaise

Even music, they say, can be political.
Think of that day in Paris—
a warm spring had brought the roses out
near the Place de Vendôme.
Gulls perched on mooring posts
watching the glassy Seine. The usual cries
of fruitsellers, the café clatter of chairs and talk
had gone, like the citizens, into hiding.
In the flats, radios whispered like parents
about a terrible storm approaching.
But one could just listen at the windows for that.
Between reports, though, a classical program—
first Berlioz, for splendor, then Fauré
who made the cello an instrument of forgiveness,
and finally Chopin, who dwelt among the black keys,
who could tell the French a thing or two
about losing one's homeland.
When the first tanks clattered into the streets,
the radios were aimed from open windows.
When the broadcast was cut,
the last piece playing was a polonaise.
Somewhere, an officer was probably laughing
at the coincidence. For the rest of the day,
the chords lingered like blue smoke.
By nightfall, they were forgotten.
Cleaning their guns in the chandeliered lobby
of a hotel that they'd seized for barracks,
soldiers whistled melodies from cabaret songs

that had just started playing

when they shipped out, months ago.

II.

What the Cave Painters Saw

How grikes must be crossed
to hide the rudiments of shadow
lodged in every shape,
that mica glistens under fingertips,
feldspar deepens, gypsum weeps
into orchids, chameleon tails, proboscides,
that draperies of rainfall can ledge
into flowstone clints, cleaving walls
bare as those clearings among pines
where all is hush and hush again.
Yet these were as nothing
to the spectral herds lurching
towards vision
through bulrush smoke and days-long fasts,
bodies hued in what must be
ground to liken such hues—
bone charcoal or woad's indigo,
powder of hematite (all shine)—
the hunger-saters,
the warmth- and tool-bearers.
Long vigils over their motions
were the first polyphonies:
why is my body I, what is not I,
what is, what is, what is.

What the Classics Teach

For thousands of years, we have searched
yellowed papyrus and smooth vellum,
human eyes bright with youth
or bleary from too many nights
reading by dim candle or lamplight,
seeking answers to ancient questions:
how to stab a man, how to die shouting,
divide a community, collapse
under the dark madness of revelation,
how to run from a burning city
while bearing your father
on a back weary from combat,
your household gods in your pocket,
your child clinging to your arm
as you rush to the safe harbor,
how to lose your wife,
while always learning how empires begin
in the loss of one's homeland,
in exile, in savagery.

Some Folks Still Live by Myth

Achilles got blown away

on a sea-blue day,

two shotgun kicks to the heart.

Ajax botched his own death,

almost, then made

a cut and a cut and a

bloody mess of hisself.

So Odysseus was damn glad

to be rid of them goons,

home a few hours

across the lazy waters

and him itching for Penelope,

with no thought whatsoever

given to honey-traps.

The Honey

Sappho understood war,
understood how
the peace of the body
is bought with years of grappling
and rude breaths blown
against cheeks so close
they touch. Yet battle
never echoes along her lyre strings,
and heroes go unnamed
in her fleeting, fading lines.
What need had she
of Achilles and Hector?
Her body was stung, she sang,
as with a bee's black thorn,
and she would lay it down
in meadows of sweet clover,
where the hive might fill to the brim
her every cell with honey.

Pomegranate

At first glance, a pomegranate
looks like it should burst
with monsoons of juice
the moment your teeth graze it,
or looks perhaps not like fruit at all
but a leathery Chinese lantern
in a restaurant run by immigrants
soon to be deported.

Yet you learn the pulpy rind
that runs straight to the heart
is honeycombed with ruby grains,
and the seeds themselves
neither gush nor overflow,
but offer a teardrop's worth
of sweetness so subtle
you scarcely notice at first.

Cut in half, the pomegranate stains
the blade and does not wash easy.
Torn, it only darkens the hands.
You have to peel away
a bit of flesh, loosen a seed,
taste, savor, repeat. To consume
a pomegranate with rightful ceremony
may take an hour of your life

or, as Persephone learned, an eternity.

The Lyre

                    feet broken

the statue
                                          eyes turned

cradled arms
                                          toward the heavens

                    at rest

                    as if awaiting

one hand curled
                                          furtherance

around a branch
                                          thin-edged leaves

                    olivewood

                    in a loop of

Orpheus
                                          endings, beginnings

is not coming
                                          for you

                    loss, O loss

                    the lyre is

he lied, my dear
                                          unbroken

the strings
                                          so he remains

                    unstrung

                    the arrow

that absence
                                          the center

draws toward
                                          full of light

                    piercing

Sloth

When, and if, we think of you,
it's like staring through humid haze
at the souls in some distant circle
of hell, perhaps, or heaven,
though it's hard to tell
with us here
so far down below,
where things get done
to us faster
than heart can feel
or mind master,
where things get done
to us, where things get done.

Mister Wind

That bare ravager of clouds, Mister Wind,
makes do with lacy jags midwinter days,
juicing up on thunderheads when spring strays
summerwards. Tornadoes rush out, ears pinned
back, eroding little towns with mom & pop
diners, six churches, and a middle school
whose misery of desks teaches one golden rule:
this hungover world runs a tight shop.

O rip it up, Mister Wind, shred each town
where flags unfurl a mythic constellation
us dumb brutes would die for. If we were thrown
a thousand miles to sea, would the nation
care one flying fuck? O Wind, tear it down,
let the doggone stars rinse our milky vision.

The Soldiers

Today, soldiers will be born,
in white hospitals or beside drainage ditches,
on lonely farms or in stalled cars,
their mothers and fathers transformed
into makers of soldiers,
whether from an act of lawful union
(a Paris hotel, the window open, stars)
or the brutal dream-fever of rape
(huts and fields burning,
the lowing of slaughtered cows).
Their faces wiped of blood,
the soldiers born this day
settle into that first sleep,
as deep as death, swaddled
in blankets of fresh cotton or dank wool.
Later, they wake with a hunger
that lasts their whole lives.
Somewhere a skyscraper shimmers,
ripples shatter the blackness of a well,
and the day swells with a clarity
of light, of purpose,
neither clouds nor birds can comprehend
as they pass through endless sky,
but that, somewhere,
stirs a newborn dictator deep in his heart,
making him shake his rattle greedily.

The Day Would Be Remembered

The phones screamed all afternoon,
family calling family,
each lover their beloved one.
The blue sky was empty,

save a few clouds that held
no promise of cleansing rain.
For an hour, each heart swelled
with grief for a stranger's pain,

then sank into silence,
lacking words to shield
a fragile innocence.
When crows at last had wheeled

home to the full-leafed trees,
life crept back in. Children
played baseball, the wheels
of a fallen bike spun

in the breeze, and those who lived
greeted others warmly.
The day would be remembered
as one when family

called family, each lover
their beloved one.
But none would forget, ever,
how the phones screamed all afternoon.

Matchwood

This Jack, joke, poor potsherd, patch, matchwood, immortal diamond / Is immortal diamond.
—Gerard Manley Hopkins

Believe you me, lightning strikes
are God's gravest blessing, the licks
a grizzly gives the hiker curled on all fours,
the kiss before he's flipped like a tortoise.

First the air parts. Yes, it parts. Gnats
know they fly through more than nothingness,
which is why their wings sing. When it's done,
clouds are a black skull you peer through, the thrown

bolt a fatal frequency we call credo.
Sure as H-E-double toothpicks, you'll know
whether to crouch under jackpines that burn
or stand in the open, like a jackpine, and burn.

Sparks rise through blood. Breath's dynamo hums.
Flagrant prairies sing the sky bright psalms.

We Have Invented Nothing

Gutturals of wind cross sandstone mesas
beneath stars blown out before their light arrives.

No egg, this geode, but a fist closed round quartz teeth.
The threat of birth excised, death never arrives.

A bright day in Granada. Lorca feels himself dissolve
as the matador lowers the muleta and the bull arrives.

Hung from bridges, bedsheets bloody with spray paint
proclaim *State Champs / Darrell Loves U / The End Arrives*.

A botfly's egg case can't be torn from the host's flesh
without infection. Its only cure: wait till the nymph arrives.

Her nipples. Catkins of birch. Pastures of vetch beyond.
Field-dressed deer wait in truckbeds as the butcher arrives.

We have invented nothing. Cave murals tell us
of unseen worlds, laws like autumn, and how the self arrives.

Quantum Novena

The terrible angels of neutrinos
hurtle through our bodies
second after second,
proof we're empty within.

But there's a force
that plays dice with our bones,
fills our nostrils
with electron clouds of incense,

and showers our eyes' dark centers
with everlasting flame.
Sweet Jesus, unholster borealis,
let the quantum burn bind us all.

Salve

The burned man dreams tears
of lanolin run down the wind-
and fire-swept steppes of his face,

purple gentian, puffed morel.
These tears swallow the tears
of pus his body weeps for itself,

staining sheets with memories
of rafters snapping like matchsticks,
the molten roof pouring in,

then the distant stars of hands
hoisting him, from out a womb
or burning coffin, he couldn't say.

The nurse assures him, regular
as a rosary, he saved the girl,
she's back with her mother, his wife

or somebody's wife, he's beyond
that now, resting in a hammock
strung between silvery aspens.

There's wind, and a dog guzzling
water from a bowl, who salves his face
with the moist rose of her tongue.

Falconry

The dead fly from our hands
the way trained falcons do,
the kick of departure
echoing in the wrist
no matter how heavy the glove.
Only when we stand in a meadow,
sun shimmering over long grass,
does the training come clear:
the hoods of darkness they learn to wear,
the brilliance when the cloth's removed,
the piercing weight we lift
level with our eyes
and fling out
with a gesture of scattering seed.

De Caelis

Sequences & ratios mark   the sky:
             (mar?)
a shriek of starlings or star of shrikes ravels
in wondrous Celtic knots, endless as π,
wind-drawn contrails whisper how our travels
cross & fade in non-Euclidean lines,
thunderheads cascade, & auroras, slick-
hued with witch oils, roil toward horizons:
page after page of heaven's arithmetic.
What's their function? A world of add & subtract?
Yearling geese fill gaps in autumn Vs,
virga fades, hail kills crops—a hard fact.
Might God in fact reside in multiples—
pollen or snow—or in dividing plague & wars,
             (reminder?)
our remainder   the space between stars?

A Conjecture Leading to a Psalm

So you doubt the whereabouts of God,
a quark, everywhere yet nowhere at once.
So the hell what? Doubt you the wind,
doubt sandstone erosion and trilobite carapace.
Let faith in dawn weather slow as feldspar.
The sperm whale's lungs collapse a thousandfold
in unfathomable depths, yet bear it, unyielding.
You who preach against miracles, go doubt
the arctic tern asleep on the wing.
Doubt that a father will leave untouched
constellations of frost inside his windshield,
the breath of his child frozen overnight.
Doubt that bodies lose a few grams the moment
of death. Doubt that, you who will, doubt that.

Sortes Alabamae

Hereabouts, kudzu runners snake up death-sentenced trees,
the trunks lost in shadow like cause the sun done quit.

You betcha possum makes good pie, baked with snap peas.
A tornado can divine the gravest questions. Go on, ask it.

As tongues of iron to the anvil, so lengths of bone to the block.
The law of diminishing returns says you diminish when you return.

A long time back, folks thought bleach cured poison sumac;
'round here, you talk healing, you first got to make your skin burn.

Where buzzards glide in great wheels, black-cowled Eumenides,
bodies once hung from branches and yowled for the light.

A billboard: *Heaven—Your Name Here*. Blessed Mother of Vacancies,
it's forty for the motel or sleep in these soybean fields tonight.

Let your tongue stitch back and forth with hers, a splice.
You'll find no ifs, and, or buts between the creeks of her thighs.

Bending the Bow

Trying to say what needs to be said
and failing. The way the light pooled
in my wife's eyes those six long minutes
we stared at each other in bed
one morning. Neither of us speaking.
When the Zen abbot was asked
how the monks proved such adept archers,
he said, *We try not to try not to miss.*

Impressions

How odd how easily one confuses them:
Monet and Manet! Nothing alike, of course,
differing not just in subject, which seems obvious—
cathedrals at sunset, lilies, and vague figures
in a train terminus on the one hand,
and on the other, crowded Parisian scenes
with whole novels inscribed on every face—
but in the striking ways that those impressions
for which they're famed are simply a matter
of where one locates the haze and motion
of lived life. In Monet's oils, the viewer's eye
is always at issue, as if the painter were concentrating
on how we see peripherally, how, at the edges,
sight is both acute and alluringly inexact,
creating an erotic moment that leads the eye
chasing after a world it mistakes for the world
it envisions. Whereas in Manet, the eye sees
with absolute clarity across the ever-present
distance between viewer and subject,
but the life it perceives is itself marginal, blurred,
transient, as if glowing faintly with a fate
one desperately longs to comprehend, but cannot,
thus creating another erotics, not of uncertainty
about all that is seen, followed by desire
to bury oneself within the truth of it, as in Monet,
but an erotics of the certainty that all is illusion
and one must play along. That woman staring out
from behind the bar in Manet's *Folies Bergères*

sees another woman's face, fleeting
as one of Monet's water lilies, and wonders
if this is evidence of the shadowy miles between lives
or of the distance she lives from her own heart.

The Book of Clouds

Thumbed through, its onionskin pages
sound the patter of summer rain.
The font is Gothic, the type miniscule,
each column of text a Jacob's ladder
leading to the chaptered heavens.
Left too long on the shelf, it thunders,
soaking the covers it's set between.
In the chronicles of cumuli, you will find
a record of those white blossoms
that floated through the blue pastures
of childhood, on long afternoons
when you could watch the sky
unfurl into castles, griffons, gods,
and behold everything in which you believed.

A Closer Absence

There's got to be a word
for this longing
that kneels beside you
in an empty chapel
or follows you beneath bare trees,
a word inflected
with pulse and handclasp and breath.

You would need a thousand tongues
just to speak it,
unless you found
you were one of the tongues
and the word
was being spoken
through you. Was you.

III.

Gab and Briar

Shagbark copses go winter to humid
in a heartbeat. What great heart, I wonder,
lies so mighty still? After each spring flood,
a contusion of buzzards bruits the air.

Between getting and begetting is lore
or love. When she did surrender her body,
a map whereon the compass rose did flower,
I told the auctioneer I'd be bidding early.

See yon haze over hills, blue as a dish?
Hear that goldfinch in the thistle? I swear
this noon sun's heavy as an angel's touch.

O, it took time to get peaceable here,
for like with Cain, the Lord didn't proffer much
but dust and honeysuckle, gab and briar.

Lentecost

Y'all fixing to die in awful ways.
Shame you can't see. Bees be helicoptoring
over clover, black bears snarl awake, ginseng
fingers up in woods where no one strays,

and still y'all sure of what the spring says:
beauty be resurrected, some such thing.
Can't see past the pear trees blossoming
to the hawk glaring from a stand of hickories.

Hunger's what it means, a famine hard on
winter's heels. No berries yet, no calves born.
This here wet breeze carries some fool notion

that life's looked after—God cares—and yon storm
ain't bringing floods, but will raise up new corn
and kindle trees with verdant flame. O yessum.

Oneliness

Into her pregnancy he did throw himself,
the taut honeydew of her waist an unspoken plosive.

When the missionary position became unthinkable,
they thought how hummingbirds can starve on the wing.

The hour the wind-lapped shingles proclaimed the hour,
her body was a battlefield reclaimed by rain;

awkward prayer did follow snippets of medicalese.
O you are so not leaving this room, mister.

Grackle eyes are thimblefuls of gold.
Imagine hearing the vulgate after a lifetime of Latin:

first creosote, then the sigh of thunder-drenched grass.
Each fingernail a moon provoking *Goddamn, I love you.*

Let there be labor both day and night during harvest.
The combines wonder at the resurrection of the wheat.

Parable, with Crawfish

It's the impurities let the crawfish
keep on keeping on in this shadowy creek.

Sure, there's slag and silage. Slurry'll splash
over dam walls or through freeze cracks leak
oil like the ooze of godlessness crushed.

But I'm talking mud and catalpa rot,
dragonfly larvae and fish bits all mushed.
I'm talking Coke bottle glass brown. Clear clot.
They favor south sides of rocks and sunk junkers.

Go slow. Spook 'em, and mudbugs'll crawl
up any tightass niche they can to hunker
deep down. Look for where fast eddies stall.

When they engravel in beds of chert,
you've got to hoke 'em out like God's own heart.

Prophecy

Where the hoochie-coochie meets the fish boil,
you'll find layers of dissonant outcomes.
But prophecy's sticky as motor oil.
Even proved wrong, a foretold truth still hums
like buglights in August. Can't shut it off.
Seems folks've always heard how they'll thrive or die
with the coming times. Sad winds hack and cough,
spit their lunged-up sickness in each man's eye
whilst sulphurous mist blinds the river delta.
How forever hated this miserable tract
where fallen fruit spoils. Some say there's hell to
pay for God-given truths the cussèd lacked
the God-given sense to ken. In the saying
is the sooth. How like the snake's hiss sounds praying.

Metonymic River

Done foresaw cottonmouths snarled in reeds,
spring gussied up in lilac finery.

A brief rain glistens upon hickories.
For rain, read sunspill; for glistens, read blisters;
for brief, read all the livelong day, sugar.

Dark corner of the whitewashed room,
so bored out your gourd you start to dream

of a lazy rope swing over the river,
bra straps snagged under a finger,
frog jelly spilt out its mason jar.

You know the shadows'll want their cut
from the heart of them Black-eyed Susans.
But sing hallelujah, the outboard's caught.
Now let's get us some catfishing done.

Axiom of Saturday Nights

Sometimes a man gets tired
of doing for others.
Then he sets off looking
for some varmint to kill,
some woman to
dance circles around.
He puts on a clean shirt,
trims the waning moons
from his fingers.
There are establishments
with such men in mind.
When he steps out the truck,
the gravel round his boots
is rhinestones glittering
under house lights.
Inside, folks bow their heads
as he passes. All can tell
a deed is beginning,
the air poised
like a nameplate on a casket
awaiting engraving.

Orchard

All night the gambrels creaked
and the orchard turned to dew.

Sugarbrains, she whispered
through the swaddling darkness,

Why do only horses have fetlocks?
He grabbed her fetlock in horseplay,

brushed back blond creeks
from her eyes so he could see

her eyes go through him like nails,
her look sullen, her desire aplenty.

Nestling close as roof to rafter,
a crop of hungers in-between,

they sought to true their lyric
bodies like air in a bevel,

so when he slipped her the tongue,
she slipped him the grammar.

Covenant

When the grackle soul rends its metal
read-a-leak, read-a-leak

and the bleb of sun casts chill
through craquelure of hickory,

let you get you good shine.
Yon lachrymose mulberry,

dead drowse of cornsnakes
lodged up under creek banks

like grit under sharecroppers' nails,
even them rickety deer, do so need song.

Howsomever you pass by, may cobweb
ever ripple with breath. Yourn.

But say you be the whisper of gas
in seed-drill engines, the pock

in lake-ice muskrats dive through.
What when spring summons strips

of oak from forest floor declivities,
spires heat columns whence buzzards

scan down blooms of winter dead,
shall you be without or within?

Scarcely here, child-of-a-season,
we never did get to tonguing your name,

though you be bespoke for, and bespooked.

Acknowledgments

Grateful acknowledgment is made to the editors of the publications in which these poems first appeared, sometimes in different versions:

32Poems: "Covenant" (originally published as "Spring Covenant")

66: The Journal of Sonnet Studies: "Matchwood"

Beloit Poetry Journal: "Oneliness," "Sloth"

The Broadkill Review: "Axiom of Saturday Nights," "Metonymic River," "Parable, with Crawfish"

The Capital Gazette: "The Day Would Be Remembered"

Cathexis Northwest Press: "The Lyre", "Impressions" (originally published as "Monet / Manet")

Chesapeake Taste: "Falconry"

The Christian Century: "A Conjecture Leading to a Psalm"

Christian Science Monitor: "Pomegranate"

Contrary: "Burning Sappho," "The Soldiers," "What the Classics Teach"

The Delaware Poetry Review: "The Hawk You See May Be Your Own," "Prophecy," "Lentecost," "Some Folks Still Live by Myth"

The Delmarva Review: "Émigré," "The Honey," "Sortes Alabamae"

The Flea: "De Caelis"

Green Mountains Review: "Polonaise"

High Shelf Press: "Southrenody"

The Humanist: "Paradiso"

Poetry Kanto: "Gab and Briar," "Orchard"

Southern Poetry Review: "Death's Sparrow," "What the Cave Painters Saw"

Spirit First: "A Closer Absence"

West Branch: "Eclogue of the Resurrection of the Wheat," "Mister Wind"

"Salve" received the Dorothy Sargent Rosenberg Prize for Poetry.

"A Closer Absence" received the Spirit First Editor's Choice Award.

"Oneliness" and "Sortes Alabamae" were nominated for the Pushcart Prize.

"The Day Would Be Remembered" was written in response to the shootings at the Capital Gazette in Annapolis, MD on June 28, 2018, and was read at a city-wide vigil on June 30.

Some of these poems were published in *Southrenody,* which won the 2019 Raw Art Review Poetry Chapbook Contest.

The Naval Academy Research Council and the Maryland State Arts Council provided grants that helped with these poems.

Temple Cone is Professor of English at the United States Naval Academy and the former Poet Laureate for the City of Annapolis. He is the author of four books of poetry: *Guzzle; That Singing; The Broken Meadow*, which received the 2010 Old Seventy Creek Poetry Press Series Prize; and *No Loneliness*, which received the 2009 FutureCycle Press Poetry Book Prize. He has also published seven poetry chapbooks, as well as critical reference works on Cormac McCarthy, Walt Whitman, and 20th-Century American Poetry. He holds a Ph.D. in Literature from the University of Wisconsin, an M.F.A. in Creative Writing from the University of Virginia, an M.A. in Creative Writing from Hollins University, and a B.A. in Philosophy from Washington and Lee University. He lives in Maryland with his family.

Also Available
from
Cathexis Northwest Press:

Something To Cry About
by Robert T. Krantz

Suburban Hermeneutics
by Ian Cappelli

God's Love Is Very Busy
by David Seung

that one time we were almost people
by Christian Czaniecki

Fever Dream/Take Heart
by Valyntina Grenier

The Book of Night & Waking
by Clif Mason

Dead Birds of New Zealand
by Christian Czaniecki

The Weathering of Igneous Rockforms in High-Altitude Riparian Environments
by John Belk

If A Fish
by George Burns

How to Draw a Blank
by Collin Van Son

En Route
by Jesse Wolfe

Moonbird
by Henry G. Stanton

Cathexis Northwest Press